SAMUEL BARBER

EXCURSIONS

for the piano

Ed. 2138

G. SCHIRMER, Inc.

DISTRIBUTED BY

HAL•LEONARD®
CORPORATION

7777 W. BLUEMOUND RD. P.O. BOX 13819 MILWAUKEE, WI 53213

These are "Excursions" in small classical forms into regional American idioms. Their rhythmic characteristics, as well as their source in folk material and their scoring, reminiscent of local instruments, are easily recognized.

Excursions

I

Samuel Barber, Op. 20

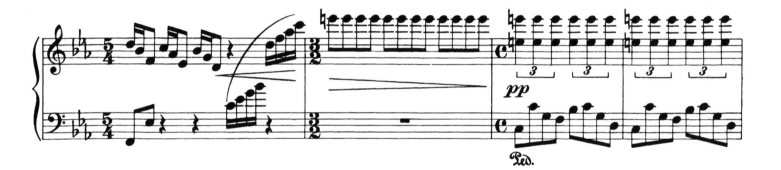

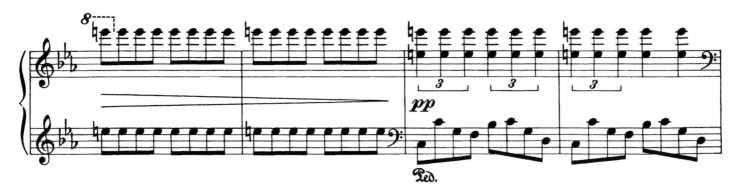

II

In slow blues tempo ♩ = 60

Piano

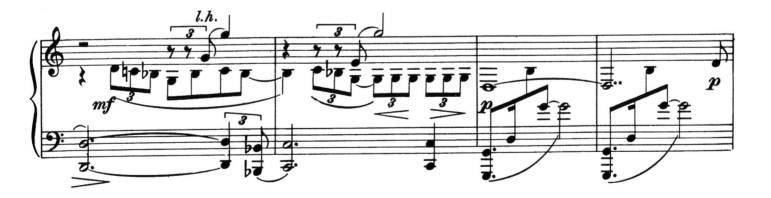

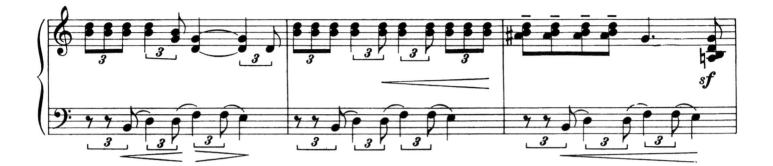

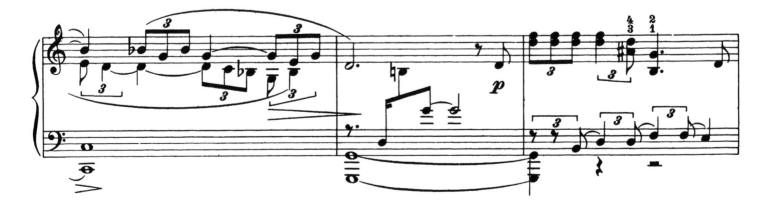

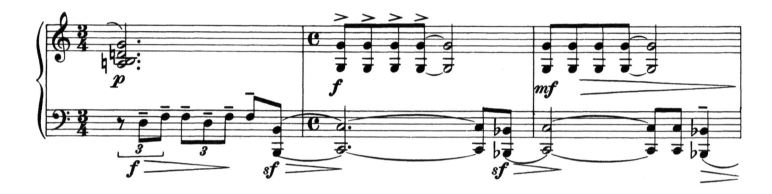

allargando sino alla fine

III

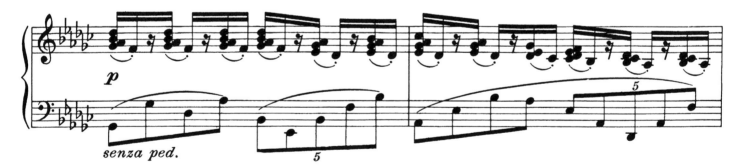

IV

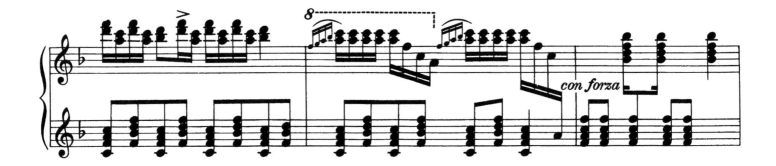

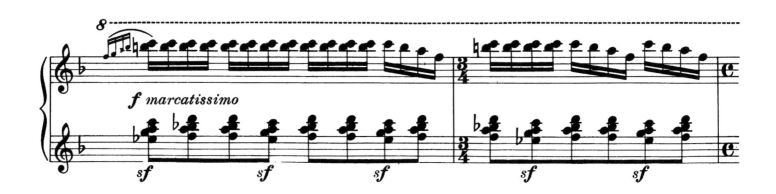

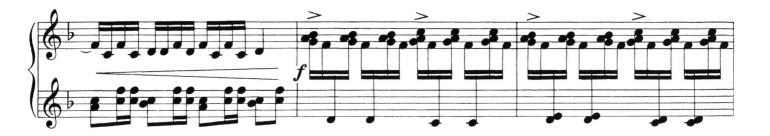

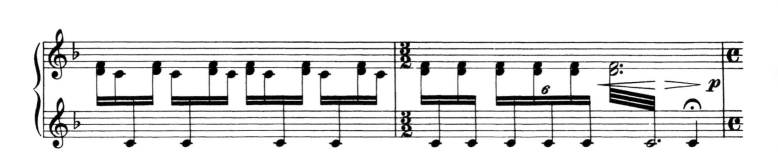

Tempo Iº